Prayer & Petition

This book on **Prayer & Petition** is part of the Ezra 7¹⁰ ™ series of publications. It is also part of a larger three-book discipleship program called the *Ezra 7¹⁰ Plan*. Specifically **Prayer & Petition** is in the *Ammo* section (being part of the *Armor of God*), included as part of Book 1 - ***First Love:*** *A Heart to Understand.* For more information about this plan please go to the program web site at http://www.ezra710plan.org

Prayer & Petition

Geoseff Obadiah Doulos

Cover Graphic: Heart_sweetheartValentine –by Jouni Paavilainen:
www.ChristianPhotos.Net

Editor-in-Chief: Judy Kissinger

Prayer & Petition

Copyright © 2010 by Geoseff Doulos
Front Royal, VA 22630

Ezra 7<u>10</u> publications
ISBN – 13: 978-0-61542-851-2
ISBN – 10: 0-61542-851-7

To the Glory of God

Contents

Prayer & Petition

The Ezra 7¹⁰ Plan *1st Love*

Prayer & Petition

AMMO

This book is part of the Ezra 7¹⁰™ Plan that includes a discussion on the full armor of God as mentioned in Ephesians 6:10-18. We have split these weapons of spiritual warfare into two groups: *Armor* and *Ammo* (ammunition). It is obvious that armor is primarily defensive as it is worn to withstand attacks. However, within the description of the *Armor of God* a few offensive weapons (*Ammo*) are mentioned such as the *Sword of the Spirit* (Word of God). We have also included *Prayer and Petition*, and the *Gospel of Peace*, as examples of offensive weapons we can use to stay on the attack. In this book we will discuss the offensive weapon of *prayer and petition*.

Ephesians 6:18 *With all prayer and petition pray at all times in the Spirit, and with this in view, be on the alert with all perseverance and petition for all the saints,*

It may seem strange to separate petition from prayer, but since the Scriptures make the separation (both Old and New Testaments), we will discuss them individually as well. Although we will discuss these two words separately, it should be noted that *prayer,* when used by itself, normally includes the idea of *petition.* While we may not have thought of prayer as a weapon, after this discussion it is hoped that our eyes will be opened to the tremendous power (and privilege) that is available to us.

This privilege needs to be accessed correctly and used properly; otherwise it will be ineffectual and worthless to us.

Prayer & Petition contains five main sections: *Intimate, Inhibit, Infinite, In to it* and *Inform it.* First in *Intimate* we look at the many dimensions of prayer and petition. *Intimate* also discusses how prayer and petition can enhance our relationship with the Lord.

Inhibit candidly talks about some common pitfalls and distractions that prevent us from praying as we should. *Infinite* discusses the amazing power that is available to us. In the next section *In to it*, we relay some very tangible ways to get started on our prayer and petition time. Finally, in the last section, *Inform it*, we talk about ways we can teach others to pray.

Remember when the disciples asked Jesus to teach them how to pray? As our prayer life increases people will notice and they will ask us about it. We need to be ready to teach, train, and raise up new prayer warriors.

Before we forge ahead we want to preface the upcoming sections with a word of admonition and encouragement. Praying effectively is not simply kneeling down and talking as some may think. There is some good in doing that. If that is all it takes, however, then Jesus would have communicated that to His disciples. In reality He gave them quite an outline of things to include in prayer, and things not to include in prayer.

In many ways learning to pray is similar to learning how to ride a bike or drive a car. For those who can do both, perhaps we think nothing of all the detailed preparations we go through before and during our voyage. In our mind we simply get on the bike and pedal. We just turn the key and start driving. Our driving is just second nature to us and we may be oblivious to the many things we pay attention to during our travels.

But let us recount our initial learning process for riding a bike or driving a car. All the seeming thousands of instructions! Sit up straight, keep your balance, don't just look down, keep your feet on the pedals, don't forget to use the brake, don't go too slowly, don't go too fast, watch out for that tree. And all the countless attempts to ride ending with the bike on top of us, or worse, with us atop a thorn bush. All the while our well-meaning tutors (read: Dad or Mom) telling us how great we were doing even as we plowed into (over) yet another obstacle requiring even more bandages. And yet, a few painful days later we were well on our way to mastering it all. Now we think nothing of hopping on that bike and going for the ride of our lives.

Such is the process of learning to pray, the right way. Initially as we read through these sections it may seem that there are a lot of things to do and things to avoid doing. But if we are patient and make it our purpose to learn, we will master prayer and thus pray like the Master.

Remember, just as there are good drivers and bad drivers, there are also effective pray-ers and ineffective pray-ers. The secret is to patiently learn all the Bible says about prayer, and then to put it into practice.

Many times the difference in skill level between two people is not necessarily in the amount of time they practice, but in how correctly they perform the exercise. Compare two athletes, two musicians, two surgeons, and two artists and perhaps the difference can be boiled down to which one not only did their homework, but did their exercises using the correct form. And while it is true, as we will learn, that the Holy Spirit does help us to pray, we must make sure that we are *in tune* with Him.

When we learn anything new it is important to practice, but practice correctly. Bad habits early on can be hard to break. So it is with prayer. The good news is that this book on Prayer and Petition is designed to teach us what to do and what not to do. Although it may seem like a lot of information to digest, once we learn to pray the right way, it will all be second nature to us.

If our prayer life seems lacking in the future we can always return and read again the truths contained in these pages. We can always improve our driving, and we can always improve our prayer life!

Intimate

Purposes of Prayer

Prayer has been defined as a conversation with God. This is a good definition and even the Greek will bear that out. The Greek verb *to pray* is προσεύχομαι (*proseuxōmai*). It is a combination of the preposition προσ (*pros*) and the verb εύχομαι (*euxōmai*). The verb without *pros* is usually translated *to pray* or *to pray to God*. The prefix *pros* means *to* or *toward* and adds definiteness and a conscious direction to our prayers. Prayer is not just talking to ourselves, nor is it wishing or dreaming. Prayer is communication with God, as if He Himself were sitting right next to us. As we pour out our soul to Him in prayer, our relationship with Him will continue to deepen.

Why and how we converse with God will differ depending on our circumstances. Let us first look at different ways we can talk to God *without asking Him for something*.

What we do	What we mean
Cry, Sigh, Groan, Weep	I am sad and I want You to know it
Rejoice, Sing	I am happy and I want You to know it
Give Thanks	Thank You for what You have done
Worship, Praise, Adore, Magnify	Thank You for who You are
Confess, Repent	I am sorry, I performed poorly, I sinned

The order of these actions was intentional in that the usual priority in our prayer life can be *me first*. After we tell the Lord about all our problems and ups and downs, we barely have time to thank, praise and just worship Him. Oh, and admitting that we blew it and sinned somehow is not usually high on our list. Before we get to the asking part of prayer (petition), let us spend some time dwelling on how to develop an intimacy in prayer that perhaps we have not experienced before.

Confession

One key to intimate prayer is to reverse the order of the above and start with confession first. This is very biblical in that to approach our Father at all, we must not be carrying any weight of sin with us. Now most people tend to skip reading the book of Leviticus, but that is a shame. This book more than most will drum in the principle that to approach a Holy God, albeit our Father, atonement must be received for any ongoing sinful thoughts or actions. We are wasting time if we have unconfessed sin on our hearts. Our prayers will not be heard.

Now some may be confused at this point. We may have thought that when we became believers all our sins were forgiven. That is true. When we accepted by faith God's plan of salvation for us we were sealed with the promised Holy Spirit as a sign of the everlasting covenant between us and our Father. We were officially adopted into His

Family for all time. Although our entrance into Heaven is assured, the relationship we have with our Father is still based on walking by faith and obedience. Sin is the impediment to our faith and obedience, and thus to a close relationship with the Lord as Isaiah says.

Isaiah 59:2 *But your iniquities have made a separation between you and your God, And your sins have hidden His face from you so that He does not hear.*

   We do not need to be perfect to approach God. We do need to have a clear conscience, or a *cleansed* conscience, because in spite of ourselves, we still do commit sin and need to ask for forgiveness. David says it best.

Psalm 51:2, 3 *Wash me thoroughly from my iniquity And cleanse me from my sin. For I know my transgressions, And my sin is ever before me.*

Psalm 32:5 *I acknowledged my sin to You, And my iniquity I did not hide; I said, "I will confess my transgressions to the Lord"; And You forgave the guilt of my sin.*

We often struggle with calling sin a sin, but we must be honest with ourselves, and not just acknowledge sin, but continue to forsake it so that we can be open to God. The Lord knows we will never be perfect, but what He wants is that we submit ourselves to the goal of being perfected by Him. If we truly agree with God that what we have done is sinful and displeasing to Him, then as we move forward we should sin less and less. Confession and repentance basically involve agreeing that God's ways are best and involve turning away from following our own ways. The Lord rejoices at our progress. We do not need to compare ourselves with others. As long as we are moving in the right direction, the Lord will take care of the rest.

So as we approach God in prayer we first make sure our hearts are clean before Him. Sadly, many continually carry around the weight of unconfessed sin, and their relationship with God suffers. Remember, God does not demand instant perfection. He does require that we confess our sins to Him. So instead of hiding our past sins from the One who knows them anyway, we should run to the

One who loves us unconditionally and is always ready to move us steadily on to perfection one step at a time. Our relationship with our Father will improve steadily as well! Keeping this in mind will keep us on our way to achieving a close intimate relationship with our God and Father through prayer.

Approaching God without sin (i.e., our sins have been forgiven and put away as far as east is from the west), gives us peace and confidence. But instead of just launching into a one-way dialogue, or firing off a bunch of requests, the best thing to do is to concentrate on the Lord first. Perhaps because we are so rushed for time, or maybe we have not been in the habit of worship, we seldom take the time to thank and praise our Father on a daily basis.

Worship

If we look at the people in the Bible who had a great relationship with the Lord, we will discover that praise for God was a regular part of their life. In the hustle and bustle of life our lives can become too *me* centered. To mimic those in the Bible who had a close relationship with God, we also need to mimic the time they invested with God. Spending time with God just praising and worshipping Him without thought to ourselves is not only personally uplifting, but faith building. It is interesting that by concentrating on God in praise and worship, we end up as the major beneficiary. But it makes sense in a way. We are magnifying God, and at the same time extolling the virtues of His counselor, the Holy Spirit who resides within us. So as we *lift up* the Lord, our Spirit, heart, soul, mind and strength are also lifted. What did Jesus say about worship?

John 4:23, 24 *But an hour is coming, and now is, when the true worshipers will worship the Father in spirit and truth; for such people the Father seeks to be His worshipers. God is spirit, and those who worship Him must worship in spirit and truth.*

Thanksgiving

The Lord does so much for us on a daily basis, and often we just do not take the time to show our appreciation. Unfortunately this bad habit of taking things for granted, or expecting things from God, can lead to downright ungratefulness. In severe cases it can lead to extreme bitterness. The Bible encourages us to be faithful in little so that we will be faithful in much. The same holds true with being thankful. Read the verses below and let us ponder how it is possible that nine of the ten people could be so ungrateful.

Luke 17:11-19 *While He was on the way to Jerusalem, He was passing between Samaria and Galilee. As He entered a village, ten leprous men who stood at a distance met Him; and they raised their voices, saying, "Jesus, Master, have mercy on us!" When He saw them, He said to them, "Go and show yourselves to the priests." And as they were going, they were cleansed. Now one of them, when he saw that he had been healed, turned back, glorifying God with a loud voice, and he fell on his face at His feet, giving thanks to Him. And he was a Samaritan. Then Jesus answered and said, "Were there not ten cleansed? But the nine—where are they? Was no one found who returned to give glory to God, except this foreigner?" And He said to him, "Stand up and go; your faith has made you well."*

Also, it is possible that we may be mad at God for some reason and do not want to thank Him or show appreciation for what He gives us. We may convince ourselves that He is mean, just like the people in the following story.

Numbers 11:4-9 *The rabble who were among them had greedy desires; and also the sons of Israel wept again and said, "Who will give us meat to eat? We remember the fish which we used to eat free in Egypt, the cucumbers and the melons and the leeks and the onions and the garlic, but now our appetite is gone. There is nothing at all to look at except this manna." Now the manna was like coriander seed, and its appearance like that of bdellium. The people would go about and gather it and grind it between two millstones or beat it in the mortar, and boil it in the pot and make cakes with it; and its taste was as the taste of cakes baked with oil. When the dew fell on the camp at night, the manna would fall with it.*

We may also compare our lives to others and our envy deceives us into thinking God is playing favorites, and unfairly blessing others above us. This will also foster an ungrateful attitude.

Matthew 20:8-16 *When evening came, the owner of the vineyard said to his foreman, 'Call the laborers and pay them their wages, beginning with the last group to the first.' When those hired about the eleventh hour came, each one received a denarius. When those hired first came, they thought that they would receive more; but each of them also received a denarius. When they received it, they grumbled at the landowner, saying, 'These last men have worked only one hour, and you have made them equal to us who have borne the burden and the scorching heat of the day.' But he answered and said to one of them, 'Friend, I am doing you no wrong; did you not agree with me for a denarius? Take what is yours and go, but I wish to give to this last man the same as to you. Is it not lawful for me to do what I wish with what is my own? Or is your eye envious because I am generous?' So the last shall be first, and the first last.*

No, my friends, we need to show thanks in all things. No matter how small, no matter what our current feelings are, no matter that another's blessing may dwarf ours. Become a thankful person. Be known as a thankful person!

1 Thessalonians 5:18 *in everything give thanks; for this is God's will for you in Christ Jesus.*

So far we have seen that our intimacy in prayer depends on who we regard as the real center of our lives. We approach the Lord through confession, praise and thanks. We can almost visualize this as first being on our knees bowed down then up on our feet, with eyes, head and hands lifted up.

Again, reading Leviticus would open our eyes to this pattern. Are we pushing the Book of Leviticus? We think so. The Lord asked that we would receive atonement for any sin first, before we would offer any fellowship, votive, praise or thank offerings. Even the New Testament bears out this principle.

Matthew 5:23,24 *Therefore if you are presenting your offering at the altar, and there remember that your brother has something against you, leave your offering there before the altar and go; first be reconciled to your brother, and then come and present your offering.*

We will discuss more on the how to's of confession, praise and thanksgiving in the Section *In To It: The Plans for Prayer*. Now that we have properly approached the Lord of Glory and have provided Him with our sacrifices of praise...

Hebrew 13:15,16 *Through Him then, let us continually offer up a sacrifice of praise to God, that is, the fruit of lips that give thanks to His name. And do not neglect doing good and sharing, for with such sacrifices God is pleased.*

... He will say to us, "Now what will you have Me do for you?"

Petition

The Lord encourages us to ask, seek and knock. Now if the Lord knows our needs and the needs of others, then why does He request that we ask Him to meet these needs? The answer is pretty obvious. He wants us to develop a habit of counting on Him for all our needs as well as the needs of others. Perhaps more importantly He wants us to recognize that He is the one who is providing for us. Our relationship with God can be cemented so close if we grasp this.

The Old Testament is chock full of stories where people were completely oblivious to God's provision. How would you feel as a parent after faithfully providing for your children year after year, then suddenly your children start giving credit to someone or something else for your gifts? For some, not only did they discount God's acting on their behalf, but actually gave other gods the credit. Or even worse, they completely rejected God's way of provision and sought welfare totally apart from God. This actually happens repeatedly in many Bible stories.

So how do we develop an ever-deepening relationship with God through petition and avoid the temptation to credit other things for what are really God's actions? How do we stand firm in faith instead of fear and patiently wait for God's provision? How do we recognize God's fingerprints on the gifts He gives us so freely?

There are many verses all over the Bible we can go through to help us here, but before we inundate ourselves with too many verses let us look at a story. If we were to read the Bible from cover to cover every year, we will notice that one story will be constantly mentioned throughout most of the books of the Old Testament and in quite a few verses in the New Testament. That is the Exodus story.

Let us recount just a small portion of the wilderness journey in Exodus and see if we can pick up a few good principles for properly, purposefully, patiently, persistently, petitioning the Lord, and for perceiving that He has provided to us His previously planned precious promises. Anyway, we digress. Let us briefly recount that classic journey from Egypt into the desert wilderness.

Let us look at the story knowing ahead of time that God will be trying to teach us the following about petition: God knows our needs and He alone will be meeting our needs; we can ask in faith and patience instead of fear; God uniquely creates situations of need where He can teach us about His faithfulness when we petition Him, and our motives in petition are important!

Even before the Israelites left Egypt they saw the awesome power of God's hand in the plagues against Pharaoh and his country. They should have realized that God was true to His word. As they left Egypt as promised, the Lord led them via a pillar of cloud by day and a pillar of fire by night. God's visible presence should have been a comfort to them, to remind them that He is near, just a prayer away. Also the Lord did two wonderful things for the people to show His utmost care for them, although they were completely unaware of it.

He did not lead them into the Promised Land the quick way following the coast through the land of the Philistines as Exodus 13:17 states,

Now when Pharaoh had let the people go, God did not lead them by the way of the land of the Philistines, even though it was near; for God said, "The people might change their minds when they see war, and return to Egypt."

He also led them on a course that enticed the Pharaoh to chase them so that ultimately Israel's most immediate concern would be erased. This clearly shows that although we may not understand the path we are on, we can be sure that God is aware of where we are and where we are headed. Unfortunately, many people on that trip did not see it that way.

Most folks who have read through the Bible recall the fact that the Israelites grumbled along their desert journey but it is amazing that many of them grumbled even before they crossed the Red Sea. If God has been faithful in the past to help us, He will be faithful in the future, even if we are in a different situation. The only way to build faith (and patience) and lessen fear is to remember each of God's faithfulnesses to us. Visualize this as stacking them (the faithfulnesses) one by one, like building the foundation of a house. If we are standing on His promises in our spiritual house, we will become stronger and stronger. We simply cannot adopt the attitude that God may fail us the next time. If we start thinking that way, we are constantly breaking the very foundation we are trying to build. We pray in faith, not in fear.

Of course God came through and parted the Red Sea and allowed the Israelites to go through. The Egyptian army was enticed and then trapped within the sea when God allowed the waters to flow back together. Thus not only were the Israelites freed from Egypt, but their enemies were destroyed so they would not have to worry about any attacks from them while they were in the desert.

So we can see that the Lord clearly orchestrated this escape for their good, but also to test their faith. Those who prayed steadfastly even though they were not sure why they were going the *long* way, were rewarded with a stronger faith and a closer relationship with God. The others probably grew angrier and were filled with more doubt because they started to think that this God did not know the best way to handle things. They probably figured that they were *lucky* to escape, and that if they had gone the *shorter* way they would have outrun Pharaoh and would have been in a much better position than they were in now. These same people probably continued to think that this God was weak because it took Him so long and so many plagues to get Pharaoh to agree to release them, and finally defeat him.

Then the Lord set up another test as He allowed them to go without finding water for three days. They came to a place they called Marah because the water they found there was bitter and undrinkable. Some of the people again grumbled at this. Moses petitioned the Lord and He showed him a tree and threw it into the waters and made the waters sweet and drinkable. Just finding drinkable water would have been nice; but it is interesting that the Lord shows them that even in the face of impending disaster (dying of thirst), he can provide a miracle (a tree, of all things, changes

the chemical composition of the water, so that
it goes from undrinkable to eminently
drinkable, even sweet)!

   Once again the grumblers lost a great
opportunity to build their faith and
relationship with the Lord. The others who
placed their faith in God were rewarded with
more confidence and patience in the Lord, not
to mention an increase in admiration and
thankfulness. They began to see that obstacles
are opportunities to see God in action. We
could go on, as this story contains many more
examples. The principles are clear. So now let
us answer the questions we asked previously.

   So how do we develop an ever-deepening
relationship with God through petition and
avoid the temptation to credit other things for
what are really God's actions? How do we stand
firm in faith instead of fear and patiently wait
for God's provision? How do we recognize
God's fingerprints on the gifts He gives us so
freely?

   We need to go to God often in prayer and
keep our spiritual eyes wide open to discern his

answers. We need to keep in memory all the many times God has come through in the past to build our faith for the future. Moses wrote a song about crossing the Red Sea. He even wrote another song before they crossed over the Jordan. That is a really good way to remember things. To recognize God we need to spend time with Him every day and see how He works with us individually. God knows what moves us and what will stop us. If we spend time each day to reflect, we will begin to see the pattern, and recognize God's actions on our behalf. This is the key to discerning answers to our petitions and the key to drawing closer to God. Let us always keep our spiritual eyes wide open so that we can recognize His actions amidst the world we live in.

We will discuss more details on the "How To's" of Prayer and Petition in the sections entitled *Infinite* and *In to it*. But now let us discuss some common pitfalls to Prayer and Petition in the following section *Inhibit*.

Inhibit

Pitfalls to Prayer

Lack of True Repentance

Sin is clearly the biggest hindrance to prayer. The Old Testament especially is full of admonitions that state the Lord hears the righteous (those who have right standing with God), and does not even hear the prayers of those who are harboring sin.

But before we move on we need to talk about this a little more. First of all it is a tremendous blessing that God gave us a way to have our sins removed each day by our confession and through His intercession on our behalf. In the Old Testament the shedding of blood through the various sacrifices accomplished this until Christ came. We can learn something of God's view of confession, repentance and forgiveness from the Old Testament.

While God commanded a sacrifice for the remission of sins, He also stated on numerous occasions the same sentiments as described in Hosea 6:6,

For I delight in loyalty rather than sacrifice, And in the knowledge of God rather than burnt offerings.

Samuel also echoes these words in 1 Samuel 15:22,

Samuel said, "Has the Lord as much delight in burnt offerings and sacrifices As in obeying the voice of the Lord? Behold, to obey is better than sacrifice, And to heed than the fat of rams."

What can happen over time, especially for a particularly difficult sinful behavior, is that our confession becomes robotic, not heartfelt and almost ritualistic. What the Lord looks for when we sin is that we first call a sin a sin. This agreement with God over our action is what confession is all about. While the Lord will indeed forgive us when we confess our sins to Him, the next steps we take are equally important. The Lord hopes that we will also decide to forsake that sin. It may take a while to completely stop, but with God's help we will stumble less and less. That is what repentance is all about. We decide to turn away from the behavior.

Jeremiah 3:12-15 Go and proclaim these words toward the north and say, 'Return, faithless Israel, declares the Lord; I will not look upon you in anger. For I am gracious, declares the Lord; I will not be angry forever. Only acknowledge your iniquity, That you have transgressed against the Lord your God And have scattered your favors to the strangers under every green tree, And you have not obeyed My voice,' declares the Lord. 'Return, O faithless sons,' declares the Lord; 'For I am a master to you, And I will take you one from a city and two from a family, And I will bring you to Zion. Then I will give you shepherds after My own heart, who will feed you on knowledge and understanding.'

Another thing the Lord hopes we develop is an abhorrence of sin, in addition to our fleeing from it. Only then will the path to that particular sin become truly forsaken. This attitude toward sin takes time, but as we draw closer to the light of our lives, we find that darkness only destroys. What we truly want is a life lived in harmony with God.

So we see that forsaking sin is a process. Let us examine two spirals, one good, one very bad indeed: the bad one first.

The Unrepentant's downward spiral

Our Status	Down-ward Spiral	What we say	What is happ-ening	What it leads to
Dusty	Confession without Repentance	We know we should do better, but...	We do not like sin's effect on us, but we do not hate the sin	Compl-acency
Rusty	Complacency without Repentance	We can justify it	Sin is not a sin, or is not that bad	Apathy
Cracked	Apathy without Repentance	It is too difficult to overcome	Sin is now beginning to control us	Depriv-ation
Broken	Deprivation without Repentance	We do not care	Physical, Financial, Personal Loss	Dire Consequ-ences

Time does not permit a lengthy discussion (perhaps in another book), but please review the above carefully. The Bible has plenty of examples of people relying on God after

repenting (turning away) to pull them out of
this downward spiral.

Psalm 34:11-16a *Come, you children, listen to me; I
will teach you the fear of the Lord. Who is the man
who desires life And loves length of days that he
may see good? Keep your tongue from evil And
your lips from speaking deceit. Depart from evil
and do good; Seek peace and pursue it.   The eyes
of the Lord are toward the righteous And His ears
are open to their cry. The face of the Lord is
against evildoers, ...*

   This is such a great verse that Peter quotes
from it in 1 Peter 3:10-12.

The Repentant's upward spiral

Our Status	Upward Spiral	What we say	What is happening	What it leads to
Clean	Confession with Repentance (Mind)	We know we should do better, and we plan for it.	We do not like sin's effect on us, therefore we plan to flee the sin	Avoid-ance of sin
Polished	Avoidance with Emotion (Soul, Heart)	We can't stand the sin	Sin is so bad, that we begin to hate it, its effects on us and on others	Abhorr-ence of sin
Gold-plated	Abhorrence with Conviction (Strength)	God's mission is too import-ant to allow sin to exist	God's mission is now beginning to control us	Abeyance of sin

To avoid the cycle of sin-repent-sin-repent, we need to plan ahead to avoid sin, and develop

an actual hatred of sin. Romans chapter six
says it well.

Romans 6:11-14 *Even so consider yourselves to be
dead to sin, but alive to God in Christ Jesus.
Therefore do not let sin reign in your mortal body
so that you obey its lusts, and do not go on
presenting the members of your body to sin as
instruments of unrighteousness; but present
yourselves to God as those alive from the dead,
and your members as instruments of
righteousness to God. For sin shall not be master
over you, for you are not under law but under
grace.*

Now that we have covered the primary pitfall
to prayer, let us look at a couple more
contained in one verse,

1 Peter 4:7 *The end of all things is near; therefore,
be of sound judgment and sober spirit for the
purpose of prayer.*

Two things are mentioned in order that our
prayers succeed: exercising *sound judgment*
and being of *sober spirit*. Therefore if we lack
these two things our prayers will become
hindered.

Lack of Sound Judgment

In 1 Peter 4:7, the actual Greek word for *be of sound judgment* is written as σωφρονήσατε (*sōphronēsate*), and is in the imperative (i.e., it is a command) second person plural form. It can be translated as: *you* (all) *think sanely, sensibly, clearly, with self-control;* as well as, *be sober-minded.* The word itself contains the Greek for *mind,* or the part of the body believed to contain thoughts, judgments, etc. *Be of sound* or *clear mind* conveys the best meaning in 1 Peter 4:7. The idea is that we are focused and thinking seriously about what we are saying. We have a proper understanding of prayer, how to pray and what to pray for. Let us see if we can discover even more insight as to how we can develop sound judgment in our prayers. Read Matthew 6:5-7.

When you pray, you are not to be like the hypocrites; for they love to stand and pray in the synagogues and on the street corners so that they may be seen by men. Truly I say to you, they have their reward in full. But you, when you pray, go into your inner room, close your door and pray to your Father who is in secret, and your Father who sees what is done in secret will reward you. And

45

*when you are praying, do not use meaningless
repetition as the Gentiles do, for they suppose that
they will be heard for their many words.*

To summarize these verses: Let us be genuine
and not make an outward show of prayer to
impress others; let us be focused and find a
quiet place to pray uninterrupted; let us be
sincere and avoid using empty words or
repetitive phrases or spiritual jargon. We
should examine our heart before we pray. We
should pray *Your will* be done, not our will as
James 4:3 says,

*You ask and do not receive, because you ask with
wrong motives, so that you may spend it on your
pleasures.*

The book of 1 John relays the same
sentiments as found in the Lord's Prayer as far
as praying with respect to the Lord's will (and
not our will).

1 John 5:14,15 *This is the confidence which we have
before Him, that, if we ask anything according to
His will, He hears us. And if we know that He
hears us in whatever we ask, we know that we
have the requests which we have asked from Him.*

Of course faith is a big factor in prayer as the Scripture says:

James 1:5,6 *But if any of you lacks wisdom, let him ask of God, who gives to all generously and without reproach, and it will be given to him. But he must ask in faith without any doubting, for the one who doubts is like the surf of the sea, driven and tossed by the wind.*

So how can we exercise sound judgment in prayer? Use the following list to remind you.

- ✓ Be righteous (no sin unconfessed)

- ✓ Be genuine (no showy display)

- ✓ Be focused (no wandering thoughts)

- ✓ Be honest (no wordy prayers)

- ✓ Be serious (no frivolous thoughts or wrong motives)

- ✓ Be trusting (no doubts)

- ✓ Be submissive (not your will, but His)

Let us move on to the next pitfall.

Lack of a Sober Spirit   .

The other term, in the Greek, *be of sober spirit* written as νήψατε (*nēpsate*), is also in the imperative, second person plural form. It can be translated as, *you* (all) *be clear-headed, restrained, self-controlled,* as well as, *be sober-minded.* While it conveys a similar meaning to *sōphronēsate*, it has a slightly different emphasis. It is perhaps best translated as self-controlled. This term has to do with keeping external influences from negatively affecting us, thus affecting how we pray. The translation of *be sober*, or *be sober-minded* is a good picture in the sense that allowing ourselves to become *drunk* will negatively affect how we pray and what we pray for. But the word *sober* may be limiting in its application, so *self-controlled* is better, in that we need to keep our self controlled from many things, not just alcohol.

Let us look at a few other verses in the New Testament that employ the use of this term.

1 Thessalonians 5:6-8 *so then let us not sleep as others do, but let us be alert and sober. For those who sleep do their sleeping at night and those who get drunk get drunk at night. But since we are of the day, let us be sober, having put on the breastplate of faith and love, and as a helmet, the hope of salvation.*

2 Timothy 4:5 *But you, be sober in all things, endure hardship, do the work of an evangelist, fulfill your ministry.*

1 Peter 1:13 *Therefore, prepare your minds for action, keep sober in spirit, fix your hope completely on the grace to be brought to you at the revelation of Jesus Christ.*

1 Peter 5:8 *Be of sober spirit, be on the alert. Your adversary, the devil, prowls around like a roaring lion, seeking someone to devour.*

We can define being spiritually sober as allowing ourselves to be physically and emotionally controlled by the Holy Spirit. This is one big way the Holy Spirit helps us in prayer. Therefore, when we are not *sober* or we are *sleeping* we are allowing other things to control our behavior. When we do not yield to the Holy Spirit, we are not taking up our cross, we are not denying ourselves, and we are not following Christ properly.

When we pray we must be controlled by the Spirit. If we are physically addicted to something it will negatively affect our prayer life. If we are emotionally controlled, by fear, anger, depression, envy, doubt, prejudice, etc., it will negatively affect our prayer life. If we are lured into the pursuit of the lust of the flesh, the lust of the eyes, and the pride of life, it will negatively affect our prayer life. All these unspiritual actions weaken our will, cause spiritual *drowsiness* and will lead to our being *inebriated* by worldliness, and will definitely affect how we pray and what we pray for.

From the above verses let us list by inference what will be lacking in our spiritual lives if we are asleep or not sober:

- ✓ We will forget to arm ourselves with faith, hope and love.

- ✓ We will not be able to endure hardships nor complete our ministry.

- ✓ We will not be prepared for action or we will rely on our own strength instead of God's grace.

- ✓ We will be more easily tricked and deceived by the devil and his ways.

We will be performing the opposite of Luke 9:23,

And He was saying to them all, "If anyone wishes to come after Me, he must deny himself, and take up his cross daily and follow Me,"

It is thus extremely important that we are self-controlled as we approach the Lord in prayer. Otherwise, our thoughts, motives and desires will be negatively affected and our prayers will become ineffectual (i.e., worthless).

Now for the good news. Assuming we are approaching the Lord wearing a white robe of righteousness (i.e., sins forgiven), with praise and thanksgiving, with a sound mind and a sober spirit, we can expect heaven itself to be hushed as the Lord waits to hear what we have to say.

Hold on to something — we are now going to talk about the infinite possibilities in prayer!

Infinite

Possibilities in Prayer

The Ultimate Guide: The Lord's Prayer

There are infinite possibilities and infinite power in prayer. The key to unlocking this potential is in the understanding of what we have been authorized to pray.

Perhaps the best guide to telling us how and what we should pray is found in what has been termed the *Lord's Prayer*. This is not an actual prayer, but more of guide on how to pray. It is found in a couple of places in the New Testament, in Matthew 6:9-13 and Luke 11:2-4. Let us look at Matthew's version in detail.

Matthew 6:9-13 *Pray, then, in this way: 'Our Father who is in heaven, Hallowed be Your name. Your kingdom come. Your will be done, On earth as it is in heaven. Give us this day our daily bread. And forgive us our debts, as we also have forgiven our debtors. And do not lead us into temptation, but deliver us from evil.'*

As we further study this, remember that this guide is from the Master. This is what He wanted us to follow. Knowing the original Greek of this passage definitely adds insight to this prayer guide. We shall break this passage down thought by thought. We will move through this quickly and provide more discussion later.

The opening sentence in the original Greek could be more literally translated as:

Our Father, the one who is in heaven, let your name be honored as holy, let your kingdom come, let your will be done on earth in the same way as it is performed in heaven.

Next we are instructed to ask for our daily bread. Again the Greek can be more literally translated as, *Give to us today what bread we need.*

Next we are told to ask for forgiveness for our debts (sins). In the Greek we find, *and dismiss our debts as we also have dismissed our debtors.* The last few words, *as we also have dismissed our debtors,* is clearly a reminder that we need to be gracious and forgive others. If we are harboring bitterness towards others, which is a sin, it will be hard for us to have a close relationship with God. He expects us to forgive others as He forgives us.

Next an often misunderstood line, but clear in the Greek, *and may You not have cause to subject us to a trial.* Basically what we are praying for is spiritual readiness. We are telling the Lord that since we are equipping ourselves with the *Armor of God* each day (for example) and are ready for battle (we hope), we have no need for testing, since we are actively engaged in fighting the good fight. The Lord may still send a test our way, but if we are truly denying ourselves and taking up His cross, the test will only serve to give us more confidence as we pass it with flying colors. If we are not battle ready, the Lord's *trial* will show us our deficiencies.

Finally ending with, *rather rescue us away from evil* or *rather rescue us away from the Evil One* (since in the original Greek there is an article in front of the word evil (i.e., *the* evil one), possibly denoting Satan (as in Matthew 13:19).

Now let us see this more rigorous translation all together now:

Our Father, the one who is in heaven, let your name be honored as holy, let your kingdom come, let your will be done on earth in the same way as it is performed in heaven. Give to us today what bread we need. And dismiss our debts as we also have dismissed our debtors. And may You not have cause to subject us to a trial, rather rescue us away from evil.

Note that the Lord's Prayer is the perfect template as we pray for ourselves but also as we pray for others. We may pray that we advance the Kingdom of God, but we can also pray that God would use our friends in mighty ways. We can pray for our daily necessities, spiritual readiness and rescue and the same for others.

The broad categories of prayer from the *Lord's Prayer* may be stated as follows:

Truly Honoring God as Holy	- *Worship*
Establishing God's Kingdom	- *Sound Judgment*
Doing God's Will	- *Sound Mind*
Daily Necessities	- *Thanksgiving*
Forgiveness	- *Confession*
Spiritual Readiness	- *Self Control*
Spiritual Rescue	- *Sober Spirit*

It is very interesting that the previous topics that we have discussed (shown in italics above) seem to line up well with the Lord's Prayer categories. So, does the *Lord's Prayer* outline the complete scope of what we are allowed to pray? A great homework assignment would be to fit verses in the Bible that command us to do or pray for something under the above categories. In this way we can see that the *Lord's Prayer* (*LP*) really does cover everything we have been authorized to pray. We have selected a handful of verses and placed them in the proper categories as an example. Perhaps some verses will fit into more than one category.

LP category: *Truly Honoring God as Holy*

1 Timothy 2:8 *Therefore I want the men in every place to pray, lifting up holy hands, without wrath and dissension.*

Acts 16:25 *But about midnight Paul and Silas were praying and singing hymns of praise to God, and the prisoners were listening to them;*

1 Samuel 2:1 *Then Hannah prayed and said, "My heart exults in the Lord; My horn is exalted in the Lord, My mouth speaks boldly against my enemies, Because I rejoice in Your salvation."*

LP category: *Establishing God's Kingdom*

1 Thessalonians 3:10 *as we night and day keep praying most earnestly that we may see your face, and may complete what is lacking in your faith?*

Jeremiah 29:7 *Seek the welfare of the city where I have sent you into exile, and pray to the LORD on its behalf; for in its welfare you will have welfare.*

Nehemiah 2:4, 5 *Then the king said to me, "What would you request?" So I prayed to the God of heaven. I said to the king, "If it please the king, and if your servant has found favor before you, send me to Judah, to the city of my fathers' tombs, that I may rebuild it."*

Judges 1:1 *Now it came about after the death of Joshua that the sons of Israel inquired of the Lord, saying, "Who shall go up first for us against the Canaanites, to fight against them?"*

LP category: *Doing God's Will*

James 5:17 *Elijah was a man with a nature like ours, and he prayed earnestly that it would not rain, and it did not rain on the earth for three years and six months.*

Acts 1:24 *And they prayed and said, "You, Lord, who know the hearts of all men, show which one of these two You have chosen"*

Matthew 26:42 *He went away again a second time and prayed, saying, "My Father, if this cannot pass away unless I drink it, Your will be done."*

LP category: *Daily Necessities*

Matthew 22:17 *Tell us then, what do You think? Is it lawful to give a poll-tax to Caesar, or not?*

Isaiah 30:23 *Then He will give you rain for the seed which you will sow in the ground, and bread from the yield of the ground, and it will be rich and plenteous; on that day your livestock will graze in a roomy pasture.*

Exodus 16:29 *See, the LORD has given you the sabbath; therefore He gives you bread for two days on the sixth day. Remain every man in his* place; let no man go out of his place on the seventh day.

LP category: *Forgiveness*

Acts 8:22 *Therefore repent of this wickedness of yours, and pray the Lord that, if possible, the intention of your heart may be forgiven you.*

Matthew 5:44 *But I say to you, love your enemies and pray for those who persecute you,*

LP category: *Spiritual Readiness*

Philippians 1:9 *And this I pray, that your love may abound still more and more in real knowledge and all discernment,*

Mark 14:38 *Keep watching and praying that you may not come into temptation; the spirit is willing, but the flesh is weak.*

Nehemiah 4:14 *When I saw their fear, I rose and spoke to the nobles, the officials and the rest of the people: "Do not be afraid of them; remember the Lord who is great and awesome, and fight for your brothers, your sons, your daughters, your wives and your houses."*

LP category: *Spiritual Rescue*

Luke 22:32 *but I have prayed for you, that your faith may not fail; and you, when once you have turned again, strengthen your brothers.*

Jonah 2:1, 2 *Then Jonah prayed to the Lord his God from the stomach of the fish,   and he said, "I called out of my distress to the Lord, And He answered me. I cried for help from the depth of Sheol; You heard my voice."*

Genesis 32:11 *Deliver me, I pray, from the hand of my brother, from the hand of Esau; for I fear him, that he will come and attack me and the mothers with the children.*

The *Lord's Prayer* really is our *Mission Statement* and our list of spiritual objectives (purposes) rolled into one. Not only is it the great sieve through which we must pour our prayers, but indeed our life's objectives need to mirror those of the *Lord's Prayer* as well.

Most successful churches (and businesses for that matter) all have a clearly stated mission with a list of goals or objectives that they rally everyone behind. Every project, plan or action taken must be sifted through the mission statement or master plan to make sure that it achieves the correct objective. If it does not it should not be pursued. The plan can also be used to spot ineffective activity. Perhaps an action was started incorrectly, and after further examination it was found lacking. That activity would then be cut.

So it is with prayer. We must use the *Lord's Prayer* to guide us to pray for what truly is in our *Mission Statement* from the Lord. Also we must remember that the *Lord's Prayer* is not a buffet of different offerings. Everything in the *Lord's Prayer* should be included in our prayer time on a regular basis. We cannot just pick and choose to complete the objectives that may be easy for us. We will mature in our prayers and in our prayer time only when we pray through all of the *Lord's Prayer* objectives.

At least two things will happen when we do this. We will become very strong in the Lord, full of faith, and fully faithful. The other is even more wonderful. We will begin to see into the very heart of our Father God. By faithfully praying for the dearest things on God's heart, we will develop a mind set on doing God's will all the time. The distinction between what is and what is not God's will become easier to recognize. No longer will we hope we are in God's will; we will *know* we are in God's will. It will be second nature. It will be that our spiritual nature has now taken control over the fleshly nature. We can now ride that bike with skill and full confidence.

This takes time. But to mature in prayer the right way, we must pray through all of the Lord's objectives regularly. If we practice this incorrectly at the very beginning of our prayer life it can lead to bad habits and confusion later in our prayer life. We can become discouraged and stop praying. Prayer will achieve its intended results if performed properly.

Notice the focus of prayer is really not on us but on honoring God, and seeking to do His will as a citizen of the kingdom of God. When we pray using the *Lord's Prayer* as our guide it also helps us achieve what Jesus calls the two greatest commandments. These two commandments are (one) loving God with everything that we are: heart, soul, mind, and strength, and (two) loving our neighbor as ourselves. So we have a tremendous opportunity through prayer to honor God, serve God, and help others, and ourselves in the process.

Perhaps there are some nagging questions such as, "I know that the *Lord's Prayer* is the perfect guide but how do I know if what I am praying for really fits into one of the categories?" For example, what one may consider a daily necessity, another may consider a luxury. Some may think they have forgiven someone, and yet in reality they still harbor bitterness. Some may think that they are establishing God's Kingdom by praying for a multi-million dollar church building. Some may think that all adversity in their life is not from God but rather from some other source. Yes, there will be confusion at times. How do we keep this confusion to a minimum? Quite simply actually: what does the Word of God say?

James 1:5,6 *But if any of you lacks wisdom, let him ask of God, who gives to all generously and without reproach, and it will be given to him. But he must ask in faith without any doubting, for the one who doubts is like the surf of the sea, driven and tossed by the wind.*

1 John 5:14,15 *This is the confidence which we have before Him, that, if we ask anything according to His will, He hears us. And if we know that He hears us in whatever we ask, we know that we have the requests which we have asked from Him.*

Luke 18:1 *Now He was telling them a parable to show that at all times they ought to pray and not to lose heart,*

If we are unsure, then we ask God for guidance. Our confidence in prayer comes from knowing that God has authorized what we are praying. So we pray, pray, and pray even more. To develop this wisdom in praying we must consistently spend time with God, spend time in His Word and spend time praying.

It may surprise us but some of the most well-known Christians in America that have suffered through various scandals have all admitted to the same problem: they simply did not spend time with God every day. Some admitted that they had not even read through the entire Bible. While it may have appeared that their ministries were growing, in fact they were building their own kingdoms and not God's. Why do we bring this up? Because it is easy to become discouraged when we see Christians we view as really spiritual *get it so wrong*. But if we go back to the basics, we can see where they made their mistakes.

One thing we should try and keep in mind as we pray. We should be careful about praying so specifically for something that we may miss how the Lord is trying to answer our true need and not our specific request. For example, we may think that the answer to our situation may be a new car, or a new job, or a new boss, or a new church. We may think we need a wife or a husband. We may think we need more play time, less stress, etc. Our mind could be so locked on one specific answer to prayer that it may miss how the Lord is actually meeting our needs. His way will actually be better, just not the way we see it. Remember, we should be of a sound mind and of a sober mind, and not let our own way of thinking limit how God meets our needs.

Proverbs 3:5,6 *Trust in the Lord with all your heart And do not lean on your own understanding. In all your ways acknowledge Him, And He will make your paths straight.*

Praying in the will of God is not a difficult thing to grasp; rather, it is a difficult thing to be *grasped by*. Many people end letters and e-mails with various phrases such as, *in Christ, in His Service, in His grip, in His grace*, but are they really living that way? If we do not spend time with God, time in prayer and time in His Service every single day, it is doubtful if we have become *gripped by God*. Our confusion in prayer may be coming from the simple fact that we do not have a *firm grip on the plow*. We have not *taken up our cross daily* (maybe weekly, maybe monthly, maybe yearly). Once we set our hearts to live each day for the Lord, amazingly this cloud of confusion starts to clear. What could not be grasped before seems almost black and white now. Prayer is a mighty weapon in the right hands, and in the right heart.

Genesis 32:28 *He said, "Your name shall no longer be Jacob, but Israel; for you have striven with God and with men and have prevailed."*

James 5:16 *...The effective prayer of a righteous man can accomplish much.*

As Jacob wrestled in prayer, so must we.

Let us move on to some practical ways to pray.

In to it

Plans for Prayer

Fix the Time and Place

Perhaps the best place to look for a plan for prayer should be the Scriptures. We first must choose a time and place. With that in mind let us review the following verses:

Matthew 6:6 *But you, when you pray, go into your inner room, close your door and pray to your Father who is in secret, and your Father who sees what is done in secret will reward you.*

Mark 1:35 *In the early morning, while it was still dark, Jesus got up, left the house, and went away to a secluded place, and was praying there.*

There are many more verses on this same theme. From just these two verses we can see that it is very important to schedule a time for prayer, and to pick a place for prayer that is free from distractions.

We need to find this time and place so that we can become habitual in our prayers. We may have to give up some wordly pleasure in the process, but so much the better, as we are pruning ourselves so that we can bear more fruit. Perhaps we do not need to give up anything per se, but rather we can work more diligently each day to free up some time for prayer. Instead of taking an hour to do something perhaps we can finish it in thirty or forty-five minutes.

In addition to our consistent time in prayer each day, we can supplement it with time throughout the day. If we find ourselves driving, riding, exercising, waiting or with a few free minutes to spare, we can commune with God during those times as well. Perhaps we will not be able to pray audibly, but we can still pray such that God will hear us. The Holy Spirit can hear our *inward* prayers and convey them to the Lord.

Provide Structure

How do we know what to pray? We should use the *Lord's Prayer* as a guide as we have already discussed. There are also some other tried-and-true simpler acronyms that others have used.

A doration   **J** esus
C onfession   **O** thers
T hanksgiving   **Y** ou
S upplication

Perhaps we can think of an acronym for the *Lord's Prayer*? The following are some attempts.

D eclare   *Truly Honoring God*
D isciple   *God's Kingdom*
D o   *Doing God's Will*
D aily   *Daily Necessities*
D ebts   *Forgiveness*
D iligent   *Spiritual Readiness*
D eliverance   *Spiritual Rescue*

Reveal	*Truly Honoring God*
Reach Out	*God's Kingdom*
Run the Race	*Doing God's Will*
Re-supply	*Daily Necessities*
Reconcile	*Forgiveness*
Readiness	*Spiritual Readiness*
Rescue	*Spiritual Rescue*

P roclaim	*Truly Honoring God*
R each Out	*God's Kingdom*
A lways in His Will	*Doing God's Will*
Y our Food	*Daily Necessities*
E rase Sin	*Forgiveness*
R eady Always	*Spiritual Readiness*
S ave Me	*Spiritual Rescue*

W orship	*Truly Honoring God*
A dvance	*God's Kingdom*
R ight Path	*Doing God's Will*
R e-supply	*Daily Necessities*
I nnocent	*Forgiveness*
O n Guard	*Spiritual Readiness*
R escue	*Spiritual Rescue*

These are just some examples. The idea is to pray thoroughly and thoughtfully. That is the key to a life of individual effectual prayer.

As we pray through the *Lord's Prayer* the Lord will bring things to our mind to pray. As we continue we will find it necessary to write things down and keep a prayer list. We can use this list to record His many answers. This will give us confidence.

Some may argue that if we keep a Quiet Time journal and a Prayer list, we are needlessly complicating things. Not true. In fact a close reading throughout the entire Bible clearly shows that God expressly asked His followers to constantly set up memorials in writing (song), and literally in stone, marking God's answers, victories, reminders and prophecies. The prophets were asked to do all kinds of things to show people God's message as a visible reminder. God wants us to record the present, so that as it fades into the past, our future will become clear, as we remind ourselves of His messages to us. Do not be deceived into thinking that recording our life with God is a needless chore. That is what the deceiver would like us to think. We may start with just a few things on our list. That will grow.

Before we talk about group prayer, one additional word should be mentioned here about praying for people's needs. From Jesus' great prayer detailed in the Gospel of John chapter seventeen, it is clear that God will give us specific people to pray for. Jesus clearly stated who He was praying for and who He was not praying for. We should not just grab a list of dozens of names and start praying. While that may seem to be a spiritual thing to do, in fact, it may not be what God wants us to do. God raised up prophets for very specific areas of ministry. So it is with our prayer ministry. He needs His prayer warriors to fight the right battles. He does not need Jonahs who go their own way and do their own thing. He does not want us to go south when He wants us to go north. If we are open to the Lord in this area and wait for His direction, He will clearly show us the who, what and where.

One final word of admonition here: it has become a disturbing trend in some churches that most of the items on a given prayer list are devoted to only a few things that are mentioned within the *Lord's Prayer*. A close examination of the prayers in the Bible would show that the vast majority of the prayers in the Bible have to do with advancing God's kingdom, and performing His will and helping others to do the same. How often do people stand up and say, *Pray for me that I would share the Gospel boldly where I work.* How often do we see requests for personal discipline, for more love, etc. As the Lord leads, we need to find out the real spiritual needs of people (in a sensitive way of course) and be open to pray for those. We have to be careful that our prayer time is not just an activity that we can *check off our list.* Prayer is a God-directed ministry that we should be excited about and actively participating in.

Group Prayer

Now some may ask about corporate prayer (prayer in groups). This is also encouraged in the Scriptures. Let us review some verses on this topic:

1 Timothy 2:8 *Therefore I want the men in every place to pray, lifting up holy hands, without wrath and dissension.*

James 5:14 *Is anyone among you sick? Then he must call for the elders of the church and they are to pray over him, anointing him with oil in the name of the Lord;*

Acts 16:25 *But about midnight Paul and Silas were praying and singing hymns of praise to God, and the prisoners were listening to them;*

2 Chronicles 6:34 *When Your people go out to battle against their enemies, by whatever way You shall send them, and they pray to You...*

When we pray in groups we may be doing so as part of a church or a specific group within the church. We may be praising God, praying for specific people, works or ministries. The above verses bear this out. The topical context of the verse in 1 Timothy is eliminating dissensions and developing unity. One of the ways to do this is through group prayer. The specific people referenced in the prayer requests of I Timothy chapter two included: *all men, for kings and all who are in authority*. James encourages the leaders of a church to collective prayer for a sick member. These are great reasons for corporate prayer. It unifies the leadership and encourages individual members of the body of Christ. The verse in Acts shows how group prayer can encourage the people praying while they are experiencing difficult times. Group prayer can also serve as a witness and lead others to Christ. Finally, the verse in Chronicles shows an example of praying together when the body of Christ, or a group within the body, sets out to accomplish a particular mission. We can clearly see elements of the *Lord's Prayer* in these prayers.

Yes, group prayer has its place. But we must remember that the group is composed of individuals. And our strength in prayer as a group grows as each individual grows. Thus each of us needs to develop a strong prayer life,

and that will help to ensure that the church as a
whole will have a strong prayer life.

Inform it

Passing on Prayer

Motivation

There are many ways to instruct others how to pray and we shall go into a few of them. Before we discuss those perhaps it is best to talk about motivating them to pray first.

As we have said elsewhere in this narrative, praying effectively is not something you master as much as it masters you. Those who have matured in their prayer life know that prayer is not something they do, but something they have become. They do not simply pray here and there; rather, prayer is so woven into their life that not to pray is not to breathe.

One of the best ways to motivate others to immerse themselves into a life of prayer is by getting them to read writings of noted prayer warriors. We have so many to choose from: George Mueller, Charles Spurgeon, Jonathan

Edwards, John Wesley, Andrew Murray,
Brother Lawrence, John Calvin, St. Augustine
and Thomas à Kempis, to name just a very few.

More recently, Edward McKendree Bounds'
(1835-1913) series on prayer has served to
motivate countless thousands to pray.
Although apprenticed as an attorney and
admitted to the bar, Bounds felt called to the
ministry in his early twenties. He was ordained
by his denomination in 1859, and was named
pastor of the Monticello, Missouri, Methodist
Church. Instead of practicing law, however, He
became a chaplain in the Confederate States
Army (3rd Missouri Infantry CSA). Bounds was
a chaplain in the Confederate States Army
during the American Civil War. He was
captured by the Union Army in Franklin,
Tennessee, and later released. (It is one thing
to pray in the comfort of a home or church, but
try it on the battlefield. Read his biography, *E.
M. Bounds* by Darrel D. King, for even more
motivation.) After his release, he strove to build
up the spiritual state of Franklin by starting
weekly prayer sessions. Bounds was an
associate editor of the official Methodist
newspaper, *The Christian Advocate*, and

compiled numerous books on the subject of prayer (most were published after his death).

The following quote is by Claude Chilton, Jr., in the foreword to Bounds' book *Necessity of Prayer*.

"Edward McKendree Bounds did not merely pray well that he might write well about prayer. He prayed because the needs of the world were upon him. He prayed, for long years, upon subjects which the easy-going Christian rarely gives a thought, and for objects which men of less thought and faith are always ready to call impossible. From his solitary prayer vigils, year by year, there arose teaching equaled by few men in modern Christian history. He wrote transcendently about prayer, because he was himself, transcendent in its practice. As breathing is a physical reality to us so prayer was a reality for Bounds. He took the command, 'Pray without ceasing' almost as literally as animate nature takes the law of the reflex nervous system, which controls our breathing." E.M. Bounds books include: *Power Through Prayer, Purpose in Prayer, Prayer and Praying Men, Possibilities of Prayer, The*

Reality of Prayer, The Necessity of Prayer, and *The Weapon of Prayer.*

We should collect a few books on noted prayer warriors that we can hand out to motivate others to a life of prayer.

Of course our own disciplined prayer life and answers to prayer that we can share will also highly motivate others. We should not underestimate this. People are motivated by seeing that we are as fervent about prayer today as we were last year or even ten years ago. They will be even more motivated by observing that what we pray, and how we live, yields results that bring glory to God. Faithful prayer, and faithful lives, will generate enthusiasm. We can count on it. We will be asked, *teach me how to pray as you pray.*

Structure

While our prayer disciples are reading the books we give them for motivation, we can add structure to their prayer time. While this time does not always need to follow a rigid framework, some structure is necessary to make sure we follow through with good prayer habits. Remember if we practice wrong, we pray wrong and our prayer life may become aimless and powerless.

At this point we can pass on a good, easily remembered acronym such as those provided in the previous section to provide structure. Or as we have said we can make up our own to pass on. And certainly we will want them to record their prayers and the answers. There are many ways to do this, especially today with many more options (digital devices) to record our prayers.

Encouragement

Finally a good way to pass on prayer, is to pray with the person you are discipling. Pray with them in a variety of settings. Pray with them in church, pray at work, and say grace over a meal with them. Sharing answers to prayer also provides much encouragement as we stated earlier.

When it appears that God is not answering our prayers we can revisit the *Pitfalls* section and make sure we are on the right track. Perhaps all that may be needed on our part is patience.

So collectively we provide the motivation, the structure, and the encouragement. What a wonderful thing to pass on — truly more valuable than gold.

To all those future prayer warriors out there,

Prayer is not something we do that is a separate activity such as playing a sport or engaging in a hobby. And it is certainly not something we just do while at church. It is our very life. It is who we are. We are children of God and we talk to our Father all the time and every day. It is no chore.

Prayer is the asking, seeking and knocking that opens the door to the most exciting life imaginable.

Bibliography

Aland, K., Black, M., Martini, C. M., Metzger, B. M., Robinson, M., & Wikgren, A. (1993; 2006). *The Greek New Testament, Fourth Revised Edition (Interlinear with Morphology)*. Deutsche Bibelgesellschaft.

Bounds, E.M. (2004). *The Complete Works of E. M. Bounds on Prayer: Experience the Wonders of God through Prayer*, Grand Rapids, Mich.: Baker Books.

Calvin, J. (1997). *Institutes of the Christian Religion*. Bellingham, WA: Logos Research Systems, Inc.

Doulos, Geoseff (2011). *The Ezra 7:10 Plan, Book 1 – First Love: A Heart to Understand*. Front Royal, VA: Ezra 710 publications.

Galli, M., & Olsen, T. (2000). *131 Christians Everyone Should Know*. Nashville, TN: Broadman & Holman Publishers.

King, Darrel (1998). *E. M. Bounds*, Grand Rapids, Mich.: Bethany House Publishers.

Kittel, G., Friedrich, G., & Bromiley, G. W. (1995, c1985). *Theological Dictionary of the New Testament*. Translation of: Theologisches Worterbuch zum Neuen Testament. (243, 284). Grand Rapids, Mich.: W.B. Eerdmans.

Louw, J. P., & Nida, E. A. (1996, c1989). *Greek-English Lexicon of the New Testament : Based on Semantic Domains* (electronic ed. of the 2nd edition.) (1:408). New York: United Bible Societies.

New American Standard Bible : 1995 update. 1995. LaHabra, CA: The Lockman Foundation.

Spurgeon, C. H. (2006). *Morning and Evening : Daily Readings* (Complete and unabridged; New modern edition.). Peabody, MA: Hendrickson Publishers.

Strong, J. (1996). *The Exhaustive Concordance of the Bible*: (electronic ed.). Ontario: Woodside Bible Fellowship.

Thomas à Kempis. (1996). *The Imitation of Christ*. Oak Harbor, WA: Logos Research Systems.

Wuest, K. S. (1997, c1984). *Wuest's Word Studies from the Greek New Testament*: For the English Reader. Grand Rapids: Eerdmans.

www.ingramcontent.com/pod-product-compliance
Lightning Source LLC
Chambersburg PA
CBHW070548030426
42337CB00016B/2409